Perspectives

Mini Beasts
The Good, the Bad and the Ugly

Series Consultant: Linda Hoyt

Flying Start
to Literacy®

Contents

Introduction

Why are mini beasts so important?

Mini beasts are small. They live in many places all around you. Some are considered cute, but many are thought of as pests. But without them, the world would most likely end.

Bees, worms, ants, beetles, butterflies, spiders, ladybirds, caterpillars – they are all mini beasts.

How can we protect them?

Save it or kill it?

Look at these mini beasts. Each of them has an important job to do. But some people might want to kill these mini beasts.

What else could people do?

Speak out!

Read why these students think mini beasts are important.

Small animals help balance the ecosystem and keep everything in check. Frogs help keep insect populations down, and flies eat up the bodies of dead animals and clean them.

Animals are equal to us, no matter how big they are or how tiny they are. Some people think that we are the upper ones and we can do anything to the lower animals, like stepping on them. Imagine some giant doing that to you or your family!

I don't like bees because they can sting, but I know they are important. They pollinate flowers so that new plants can grow. Without bees, we would not have plants – and without plants, we would not have any food at all.

Last year, we had termites in our house. Mum and Dad were really worried. Mum said they couldn't hurt us, but they could damage our house, so we had to get rid of them.

Insect invaders

Written by Joshua Hatch

Is it ever okay to wipe out a species? Is it okay to remove a species from an ecosystem? These sound like terrible ideas because we worry about all kinds of wildlife becoming extinct.

When might it be a good idea to remove a whole population of mini beasts from an ecosystem?

Fire ants

Fire ants originally came from Brazil and Argentina. Over time, they have been transported – usually by accident – to other countries. In 2001, they were discovered in Australia at the Port of Brisbane. They probably came from a cargo ship that docked at the port many years earlier.

Fire ants damage crops on farms. These ants eat seeds, roots, shoots and even the fruit that farmers are trying to grow. Sometimes, ants do so much damage to fields, farmers can't grow as many crops.

Since 2001, Australia has worked to kill all fire ants. The ones at the Port of Brisbane have all been killed. But more remain in nearby towns – at least for now.

Wildlife is in danger from fire ants, too. Fire ants destroy the eggs and eat the chicks of birds that build their nests on the ground.

These insect invaders push native ants out of their habitat. Imagine if a stranger kicked you out of your home – that's just what these fire ants do! They can hurt and even kill people.

And here's something you would never guess – fire ants are attracted to electricity! In fact, fire ants will chew through wires and electrical equipment. This causes major damage.

Fun fact

The biggest killer of fire ants is the phorid fly. These flies don't eat the ants. Instead, they lay eggs on them. When the eggs hatch, the larvae kill the ants.

It's true that fire ants can do some amazing things. They build mounds to live in that sometimes stand 60 centimetres tall. They communicate through smell. And they build huge ant-rafts to float on water. To build a raft, they hold on to each other and create a mass of floating ants. They have wax on their bodies that stops them from getting wet.

Even though fire ants are interesting creatures, they cause a lot of damage when they move into a new environment such as Australia. So, is it right to wipe them out from these new places? What do you think?

Apology to insects

Written by Michael Leunig

Why do you think we need to apologise to insects?

APOLOGY TO INSECTS

Dear little ant, what have we done to you?
We did not understand the work you do;
The life you bring, the magic you provide,
Instead we sprayed you with insecticide.
We killed the bugs, we killed the land,
We kill the things we do not understand.
We're sorry life has got so sad and sick,
We just don't understand what makes us tick.

Leunig

How to write about your opinion

State your opinion

Think about the main question in the introduction on page 4 of this book. What is your opinion?

Research

Look for other information that you need to back up your opinion.

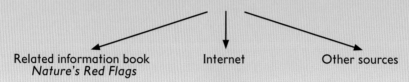

Related information book	Internet	Other sources
Nature's Red Flags		

Make a plan

Introduction

How will you "hook" the reader to get them interested?

Write a sentence that makes your opinion clear.

List reasons to support your opinion.

Support your reason with examples.	Support your reason with examples.	Support your reason with examples.

Conclusion

Write a sentence that makes your opinion clear. Leave your reader with a strong message.

Publish

Publish your writing.

Include some graphics or visual images.